THE LIFE
AND PRAYERS OF
SAINT PAUL

About Wyatt North Publishing

Wyatt North Publishing is a boutique publishing company. We always provide high quality, perfectly formatted, Books.

All of our eBooks include a Touch-or-Click Table of Contents, allowing easy and instant access to each section.

We guarantee our Books. If you are not 100% satisfied we will do everything in our power to make you happy. Visit WyattNorth.com for more information. Please feel free to contact us with any questions or comments. We welcome your feedback by email at info@WyattNorth.com.

Foreword

There are a great many men and women who have forever influenced and changed the course of Christian history, but one might ask whether any have made such a profound impact as Saint Paul the Apostle.

It is through the ardent work of Paul that we know the path to Salvation, one which leads us and binds us to God through the love of Christ.

When Jesus revealed himself directly to Paul and called Paul into his service that set Paul apart from other disciples who had come into the faith since the crucifixion.

Paul was not merely chosen to be a disciple, he had been appointed by Jesus himself.

Touch-or-Click Table of Contents

About Wyatt North Publishing..3

Foreword...4

Quick Facts...6

The Life of Saint Paul..8

    An Introduction to His Life...9

    The Early Life of Saint Paul..14

    Paul's Damascus Experience...20

    Paul and the Twelve..26

    Paul's Missionary Work 32

    Paul's Controversies...38

    Paul's Final Years...45

    From Greek Apostle to Roman Saint..51

Prayers to Saint Paul..55

    Prayer for Priests 56

    Prayer for Priests II...58

    Prayer for Priests III..60

    Prayer for Patience..62

    Prayer for Inspiration...64

    Prayer for Action...66

Quick Facts

The new "Quick Facts" section in **The Life and Prayers** collection provides the reader with a collection of facts about each saint!

Born:

c.3 at Tarsus, Cilicia (modern Turkey) as Saul

Died:

beheaded c.65 at Rome, Italy

Memorial:

25 January (celebration of his conversion)
16 February (Saint Paul Shipwrecked)
29 June (celebration of Saint Peter and Saint Paul as co-founders of the Church)
18 November (feast of the dedication of the Basilicas of Peter and Paul)

Attributes:

book
sword
man holding a sword and a book
man with three springs of water nearby

The Life of Saint Paul

An Introduction to His Life

There are a great many men and women who have forever influenced and changed the course of Christian history, but one might ask whether any have made such a profound impact as Saint Paul the Apostle.

Saint Paul's view of what it means to be a Christian, through his many letters, has been made canon, bringing his words to new generations of Christians for millennia to follow. Now that his words are canon, it is easy to imagine Paul as a mere compiler of Christian tenets, but Paul's influence goes far beyond his words.

Paul did not merely write down what being a Christian meant to everyone, he wrote down what it meant to him – and Paul was a controversial figure who shook the not yet settled foundations of the early Church. He was a proponent of intense change, and if it cannot be said that he took a small Middle Eastern sect and made it a blossoming Roman religion, it must at least be said that he worked fervently for the changes that made such growth possible.

It is through the ardent work of Paul that we know the path to Salvation, one which leads us and binds us to God through the love of Christ.

Saint Paul's influence can be felt throughout all of Christendom, but his story can also be very touching on a personal level. He was a very unlikely apostle, a persecutor of Christians who had a profoundly powerful experience and was symbolically born again through Christ, casting off his hatred in favor of love.

When we seek to know Paul through his life and deeds, rather than through his beliefs alone, we find him in canonical, as well as apocryphal and historical sources. Naturally, there are numerous quite complete explorations on the life and legacy of Saint Paul, including the inspiring Saint Paul by Pope Benedict XVI, but these are usually medieval or modern in origin and use sources that are equally readily available to us. As we seek Paul, we will consider the contemporary and near-contemporary sources first.

The canonical sources begin, chronologically, with the Pauline epistles. These are the letters that Paul sent to various congregations that he had helped develop, often to instruct them on matters of good Christian conduct. We know them, named after their recipients, as: the Epistle to the Romans, the First Epistle to the Corinthians, the Second Epistle to the Corinthians, the Epistle to the Galatians, the Epistle to the Ephesians, the Epistle to the Philippians, the Epistle to the Colossians, the First Epistle to the Thessalonians, the Second Epistle to the Thessalonians, and the Epistle to Philemon.

Of these, the letters to the Ephesians, the Colossians, and the second letter to the Thessalonians are sometimes thought by modern Biblical scholars to have been written by someone else. Traditionally, the First Epistle to Timothy, the Second Epistle to Timothy, and the Epistle to Titus , sometimes also the Epistle to the Hebrews, have been considered the works of Paul, but today many Bible scholars believe them, based on their content and language, to be later works of someone else merely attributed to Paul.

The Pauline epistles are chronologically followed by the Acts of the Apostles, although this book actually precedes Paul's letters in the Bible. The traditional view is that this work was written by Luke the Evangelist, a friend of Paul's. On this matter, modern scholars are more or less evenly divided. If it is written by Luke, it may date as early as the 60s AD, around or just after the death of Paul. If it is the work of another author, it may have been written as late as 100 AD, but with the help of a source that was present during Paul's travels. As a source for the life of Paul it is the most complete, but it can be a complicated work. It does on occasion directly contradict Paul's own writings. At other times, the historian may ask whether its details are plausible events or a literary device, and indeed whether the author's goal is not to aggrandize Paul and draw a parallel to the life of Christ. These are questions that the reader must ask, and come up with their own answer.

Outside of the canonical sources, we find several apocryphal as well as gnostic texts. The earliest work dedicated to the life of Saint Paul was written between 160 and 190 AD, and is mentioned by the famous 2nd century Christian author Tertullian. It was called the Acts of Paul and comes down to us, in its entirety, only in fragments.

Its main constituent parts, however, were so popular individually that they were often copied and distributed on their own. They are the Acts of Paul and Thecla, and the Martyrdom of Paul. In addition to these

12

two works, the Acts of Paul consist of letters and prayers, as well as several shorter narratives of Paul's preaching and miraculous healings.

Several sources on Paul's life hail from the 4th century. The Acts of Peter and Paul, and the very similar Passion of Peter and Paul, details Paul's journey to Rome and his eventual death there.

Those are the sources that deal directly with the life of Paul the Apostle, although small details can of course be gleaned from other sources as well and those will not be forgotten.

The dedicated seeker of Paul will also find several letters, including a fourth century forgery of the very warm correspondence between Paul and the Stoic philosopher Seneca, and prayers, as well as two travels to Heaven: the Apocalypse of Paul, a Catholic account that appears to have inspired Dante's Inferno, and the Coptic Apocalypse of Paul, a Gnostic text.

But for now we will occupy ourselves with the earthly life of Paul the Apostle, that begins with conception and ends, somewhat uncertainly, in death.

The Early Life of Saint Paul

Very little is known about the early life of Saint Paul. We do not know exactly when he was born or who his parents were. We do not know of his childhood exploits, or his relationship to his family and teachers. But there is much that we can infer from the little details given, primarily, in the New Testament.

The year of Paul's birth can only be derived from the dating of his letters, through references to historical people and events, and educated guesses about Paul's age when writing them. Most likely, he was born sometime around 3-10 AD. The Bible tells us that he was born in the city of Tarsus.

Tarsus lay, as is stated several times in the Acts of the Apostles, in Cilicia. It was a region of modern Turkey whose cities had been culturally Greek since Alexander the Great took it from the Persian Empire in 333 BC. By the time that Paul was born there, it had been annexed by the Roman Empire, and then largely abandoned again to be ruled by local princes and priests.

Much of Cilicia was considered hostile outback by the Romans, but Tarsus itself was a bustling capital. The city was a prosperous center for textile production, in particular the goat-hair cloth, called *Cilicium* after the region, that the Romans imported for tent-making.

The Greek geographer Strabo, an older contemporary of Saint Paul, wrote that "the people at Tarsus have devoted themselves so eagerly, not only to philosophy, but also to the whole round of education in general, that they have surpassed Athens, Alexandria, or any other place that can be named where there have been schools and lectures of philosophers."

But, Strabo also wrote that Tarsus was different from other scholarly cities in that the people of Tarsus tended to complete their education elsewhere, and then rarely go home again. Of this, we shall see, Paul is an excellent example.

The language used in Paul's letters make it clear that Paul spoke Greek on a native level, as might be expected of a man from Tarsus. He read and quoted from the Old Testament in its Greek translation, and used the rhetorical and oratory clichés of the eastern Roman schools. He was clearly at home in the Greek world and often made references to elements of a wholly Greek culture.

He was also a Jew. In Philippians 3 he tells us that he was of the Tribe of Benjamin, circumcised on the 8th day after his birth as per Jewish law. The multiple layers of cultural identity can seem positively modern, but in the same way that Polish Jews might have banded together in the United States after the Holocaust or Italian Americans may long have stayed true to their culture and language while also being Americans, so was the ancient world full diasporic communities with several simultaneous cultures.

In addition to being a culturally Greek Jew, Paul might have been a Roman citizen. In Acts, he calls upon his Roman birthright twice, but many historians doubt the veracity of these passages. However, there are several problems with the idea that Paul was a Roman citizen.

First, the way this is presented in Acts appears to be a literary device to add suspense; many readers find it improbable that Paul should wait until after he has been mistreated, even brutally beaten, for a long time to mention to anyone that he is a Roman citizen, and then even more unlikely that everyone should then believe him and fall over themselves to do him right.

Second, Paul's Roman identity appears to be used in an attempt to aggrandize Paul; he is very clearly made out to be more legitimately Roman than even the Romans themselves. Third, it is very unlikely historically speaking that Paul should be a Roman; less than 1% of the inhabitants of the Roman Empire were in fact citizens and Paul was a Jew from merely a formerly Roman fringe area.

Finally, Paul himself never mentions this improbable citizenship in any of his own writings. This, of course, does not mean that Paul could not have been a Roman. Improbable things do happen, and truths too can be unveiled at opportune moments.

More certain is Paul's identity as a Pharisee, which he tells us of himself in Philippians 3. The Pharisees were a school of thought, as well as a social and political movement, that, among other things, wished to expand observance of the Torah into the daily lives of common people, not merely the priests, and believed in the bodily resurrection of the righteous dead in the age of the Messiah. Acts 22 tells us that Paul received his Pharisaic education from Gamaliel the Elder, a highly celebrated scholar of Jewish Law in Jerusalem. Most likely, this education started when Paul became a Bar Mitzvah, a son of the law, at the age of 13.

With these many different identities in mind, we will consider one of the best known ideas of Paul's young life: his name was Saul. There is an old tradition that maintains that Saint Paul was originally Saul the Jew, and on the fateful day that he converted to Christianity he became Paul the Apostle. This is not really supported by the Bible. In Acts we find that Paul is called Saul even after his rebirth as a Christian. Having considered already his many identities, it is perhaps possible that Saul and Paul were two names that co-existed and were used both within different contexts. This was certainly the case of many immigrants in the Greek and Roman world, and it is certainly the case of many people in the Bible.

The only direct reference to Paul's family comes from Saint Jerome, who tells us that there was a tradition among Christians in Jerusalem that Paul's parents came from the city of Gischala in Galilee, but were forced to flee to Tarsus when Gischala was devastated by the Romans. If Paul were indeed a Roman citizen, this tradition cannot be true. A Roman citizen would not need to flee a Roman invasion. Curiosity also raises the question: which devastation of Gischala did the parents of Paul flee from? Gischala was still one of the last Jewish strongholds during the First Jewish Revolt, after Paul's death.

18

Paul's education, both his studies with Gamaliel the Elder and his apparent studies of Greek oratory and playwrights, however, indicates a relatively wealthy family. It is quite possible that they had slaves, including a *pedagogos* whose duty it would be to oversee young Paul's education and accompany him in Jerusalem. The family wealth most likely came from trade; as a missionary Paul supported himself as a traveling artisan. The trade, which he would have learned from his father, Acts 18 tells us, related to tent-making. Perhaps he was skilled in working leather, textiles, or wood.

The education afforded by the family's wealth is probably what set Paul off on the destructive path of his youth. Like so many Pharisees, Paul must have felt that the inclusion of Gentiles, that is uncircumcised foreigners, into Synagogues by sectarians following a Jesus of Nazareth was highly problematic and divided not only congregations, but also families. He grew incredibly hostile towards these sectarians, and campaigned vigorously to eradicate them. He even received authorization from the priests in Jerusalem to go to the city of Damascus, where there were many Jesus followers at the time, and bring them back in chains.

Paul's Damascus Experience

Of all the events in Paul's life, the one with which most people are familiar is his experience on the road to Damascus. Even so, this is one event that Paul himself says nothing about. Our main source is <u>Acts of the Apostles</u>.

Having received the authorization from the priests at Jerusalem to imprison the followers of Jesus Christ in Damascus, Paul set off for the city with a number of traveling companions.

It was a long road to travel, but as they were nearing the city one day, at midday, when Paul saw a light that shone much brighter than the sun had ever shone. It shone around him, and around his traveling companions. They all fell to the ground, and Paul could hear an unfamiliar voice speaking to him in Hebrew.

The voice said: "Saul, Saul, why are you persecuting me? It is hard for you to kick against the goad." Paul responded: "Who are you, sir?"

The voice said: "I am Jesus the Nazorean whom you are persecuting."

We have no way of knowing what Paul felt in this moment, or what he believed. He knew that the Jesus, whose followers he was persecuting, was dead. Did he know about their belief in a resurrection? Paul's experience took place not very long after the crucifixion of Christ, so the tenets of this small new sect may not have yet been widely known, but on the other hand Paul had watched Saint Stephen being martyred for blasphemy, a trial which must have brought to light many of the early church beliefs.

If he was unaware of their faith in a Risen Christ, he must have been aware of their faith that Jesus was the Son of God and his presence in Heaven. Such knowledge may explain Paul's apparent acceptance that the voice was indeed Jesus, a man he knew to be dead.

"What shall I do, sir?" Paul asked, and the voice commanded: "Get up and go into Damascus, and there you will be told about everything appointed for you to do."

However, Paul could not rise from the ground or go into the city on his own, for the brilliant light had completely blinded him. He opened his eyes and he saw nothing.

He had to be led into the city by his companions, and for as long as he was blind he did not eat nor drink.

In Damascus there was a disciple of Jesus called Ananias. After Paul had been blinded, the Lord spoke to this disciple through a vision. The Lord told him "Get up and go to the street called Straight and ask at the house of Judas for a man from Tarsus named Saul. He is there praying, and [in a vision] he has seen a man named Ananias come in and lay [his] hands on him, that he may regain his sight."

However, Ananias knew Paul well by reputation and he feared the imprisonment and potential death that would follow meeting such a man. So, the Lord told Ananias: "Go, for this man is a chosen instrument of mine to carry my name before Gentiles, kings, and Israelites, and I will show him what he will have to suffer for my name."

Ananias did what he had been told. He laid his hand on Paul and he told him: "Saul, my brother, the Lord has sent me, Jesus who appeared to you on the way by which you came, that you may regain your sight and be filled with the holy Spirit."

Immediately, Paul regained his sight and Ananias said: "The God of our ancestors designated you to know his will, to see the Righteous One, and to hear the sound of his voice; for you will be his witness before all to what you have seen and heard. Now, why delay? Get up and have yourself baptized and your sins washed away, calling upon his name."

Although the outlines of Paul's Damascus experience in Acts 9 and Acts 22 are roughly the same, they differ in the details. It would seem as if though the two accounts came from two similar but slightly different sources. The dialogue differs in content, and in some details the two accounts are even completely contradictory.

This is the case of Paul's companions. In Acts 9, Paul's companions could hear the voice of Jesus, but were confused as they could not see what Paul was seeing. In Acts 22, Paul's companions were awed by the same vision that Paul was experiencing, but they were confused because they could not hear the voice of Jesus.

How would Paul himself have understood the incident on the road to Damascus?

Although today we call it a conversion experience, it is not certain that Paul himself would have felt the same way. He never referred to it as such. In Paul's own words, he was "taken possession of by Christ."

Many historians feel that Paul did not speak of conversion in the sense that we speak of it today because "being taken possession of by Christ" did not mean a tremendous change in Paul's life. Certainly, joining those whom he had wished dead as an adjustment, but they argue that when it came to Paul's philosophy, his eschatology, that is to say: his belief in Judgment and Paradise, and the way in which his religion expressed itself physically, Paul was very much the same man before and after his Damascus experience. They say that Paul was very much a Pharisee when he started walking to Damascus, and he was very much a Pharisee on the day he died, although he had come to feel that the Messianic Age had already been ushered in.

Others have understood Paul's experience as less of a conversion and more as a rebirth through Christ. Pope Benedict XVI is among them. He sees Paul's transformation as a death of one existence, symbolized through his blindness, and the birth of another, when the Lord once again opened his eyes. A conversion, the Pope maintains, is a psychological maturation and a development of the ego through human effort — Paul's experience at Damascus contained none of these ingredients.

As one considers Paul's experience on the road to Damascus as a conversion, it is easy to get lost in the maze of personal implications, what this intimately would have meant for Saint Paul. A perhaps even more important aspect is its very public implications for the whole of the Christian community.

When Jesus revealed himself directly to Paul and called Paul into his service that set Paul apart from other disciples who had come into the faith since the crucifixion.

Paul was not merely chosen to be a disciple, he had been appointed by Jesus himself.

That made Paul an Apostle, every bit as legitimate as the Twelve in Jerusalem.

Paul and the Twelve

Having turned his hate of Christ into love, the 25-30 year old Paul went away to Arabia. He does not tell us what he did there, but there are some who have speculated that he went to Mount Sinai to meditate on his revelation on the road to Damascus. In any case, after an uncertain amount of time, he returned to Damascus and began to proselytize.

These earliest attempts of Paul to preach his understanding of the Gospel appears to have incited hatred among Jews and Pagans alike, so much so that they plotted to kill him, according to Acts 9. Paul's own version of the story, which he presents in 2 Corinthians 11, tells us that it was on behalf of King Aretas that he had to flee.

King Aretas was the Nabatean king who, only three years after Paul's Damascus experience, seized Damascus from Herod Antipas, the Roman client king of Galilee and Perea. Anyone siding with Herod Antipas might very well have been executed, and it is possible that this played into why Paul could not stay in Damascus. The end result was the same. Paul's supporters went with him to the city gates in the dead of night and lowered him down outside of the city in a basket, or took him down to the harbor and sent him off, depending on the version.

It was then that Paul decided to go to Jerusalem in order to meet the original apostles, and to learn more about the earthly life of his Savior.

It may strike us as curious that Paul waited several years to visit Jerusalem. If he had indeed been called by Jesus to become an Apostle in every right, why would he put off seeing for himself the leaders of the community, who knew Jesus in his life, and who like Paul had seen him after the resurrection?

Why would he begin spreading his Gospel, before speaking to the primary authorities? Paul was, after all, not adverse to the long travel to Jerusalem or to present before religious authority, he had done both several times.

The answer might lie, at least in part, in Paul's personal history with the Jesus movement. The letters of Paul and Acts would indicate that Paul was well known in the still fairly small Jesus community for his persecution among the early followers of Jesus.

Another reason for Paul's delay may be his awareness of the controversial nature of his claims to an apostolic calling. Although Paul recognized the special rank of the Twelve within the early Christian community, he considered himself an Apostle in the same strict sense. He had been chosen by God's grace to be a messenger of the Gospel, and Jesus had appeared to him to pick him for this task. That the original Apostles had been chosen by Jesus during his life and mission mattered little to Paul.

These claims were viewed as terribly disrespectful by many in Paul's time, and dishonest by many others. Throughout his life, Paul would come to deal with the accusations that he was an Apostle only by the grace of Satan. He must have had some inkling as to how his claims would be received in Jerusalem.

In the end, however, we cannot know the thoughts that went through Paul's head in those early days of proselytizing. But, three years after being taken hold of by Christ he arrived in Jerusalem.

Once Paul arrived in Jerusalem, he tried to join the community of disciples there, but they would not meet with him. His reputation as a persecutor of Christians preceded him and they did not feel that he could be trusted. It was not until a Levite from Cyprus, known most often by the name of Barnabas, took him under his wing, and introduced him to the Apostles that Paul gained some initial acceptance in the community in Jerusalem.

Barnabas spoke well of Paul, and of "how in Damascus he had spoken out boldly in the name of Jesus." In Jerusalem, Paul continued to speak out boldly in the name of Jesus, which may be why he was finally allowed to meet some of the original Apostles.

It is not certain that Paul met with *all* of the Apostles while he visited Jerusalem, but it is clear that he met with Peter, and stayed for fifteen days with him at his home. He also met with James.

So, was Paul's visit to Jerusalem a fruitful one, and did the Twelve accept his apostolic claim? Scholars are very divided on the question. One school of thought, to which the Pope belongs, feel that there was much accord between Paul and the Twelve, even though they would later sometimes disagree on the details of their Gospel.

Another school of thought feels that there was intense tension between Paul and the Twelve. They point, amongst other things, to the shortness of Paul's visit, and the animosity with which they sometimes opposed each other. Although Paul and Peter would often clash, they say, it was Paul's animosity with James that was the greatest.

Paul did not stay long in Jerusalem. When he had met with Peter and James, he seems to have returned to Tarsus, for what may be the first extended time since he left at thirteen to study in Jerusalem. His stay there was not long, however, because Barnabas, the Levite who had vouched for Paul in Jerusalem, was heading to Antioch on the Orontes to preach the Gospel there. On his way there, he stopped in Tarsus and invited Paul to join him. And so Paul came to Antioch, an increasingly important center for Jesus followers with a sizable community. It was there at Antioch that the followers of this fledging young religion were first called Christians.

It is difficult to say whether Paul indeed learned much about Jesus and the message of the Messiah from the Twelve and the community in Jerusalem. His knowledge of Jesus and of Christian life may just as well have come from his friends at Damascus and at Antioch. What is clear is that, even in these early years before the writings of the Evangelists, Paul was aware of many stories circulating about the life of Jesus and his words.

Paul invokes several times in his writings the words of Jesus.

Sometimes he quotes the teachings of Christ directly, at other times he uses the words of Christ in very subtle ways. For example, he portrays the ideal Christian relationship to God using the word "Abba," a somewhat childish Aramaic word that means "Daddy," that Jesus reportedly cried out to God on the eve of his crucifixion. Paul's audience did not generally speak Aramaic, so his use of the word can only have been meant to evoke Christ's relationship to God. Outside of Paul's writings, this word appears only in the Gospel of Mark, which did not yet exist.

Paul's Missionary Work

The community of Christians that Paul and Barnabas found at Antioch was probably a typical one. These communities consisted of Jews, who lived according to the covenant and the law of Moses, who went to synagogue in order to worship, to study the Torah, and to communicate with other Jews, and to spread the word about Jesus, the Messiah.

There may have been Gentiles there, people who were not ethnic Israelites, who feared the Lord and wished to worship Him. Some of them might have converted fully to Judaism, been circumcised and followed the laws governing matters such as marriage, food, and ritual purity. Many of them were no doubt uncircumcised polytheists, who worshiped other deities but were increasingly becoming involved with the God of the Hebrews.

When they partook in purely Christian meetings, they would leave the synagogue and gather instead in the home of one of the congregationalists, where they could pray together, learn together, and share in the earliest truly Christian ritual: the Holy Communion, which in those days was celebrated through the sharing of a ritual meal.

When Paul and Barnabas had been proselytizing in Antioch for only a year, a great famine struck in Judea. The Christian community at Antioch decided to send financial relief, and so they did in the care of Barnabas and Paul.

After finishing their relief mission, Acts 12 tells us, Paul and Barnabas carried on to Jerusalem, taking with them Mark the Evangelist, a cousin of Barnabas. Unfortunately, Acts does not tell us of the nature of their visit to Jerusalem, and the opening of the next chapter places Paul and Barnabas back in Antioch. There, during worship, of which kind it is uncertain, although fasting was certainly involved, the Holy Spirit came to the prophets and teachers at Antioch and told them: "Set apart for me Barnabas and Saul for the work to which I have called them."

So began Paul's life as a traveling missionary, at the age of 40-45. It is clear from all the writings about Paul that from around 47-48 AD, until his death, Paul spent his time supporting and developing the budding Christian communities around the eastern Mediterranean. In some communities he stayed a few weeks, in others he stayed for years.

Painting a picture of Paul's travels, however, and especially a chronology, comes with great difficulties. The traditional view, derived from Acts, is that Paul went on three grand and carefully planned missionary tours, which can be found in Acts 13-14, 15-18, and 18-21.

The image that comes out of Paul's letters, many of which were composed during his travels, is rather different. Not only is it impossible to detect these three grand tours, but the Paul of his letters do not appear to have taken the same routes as the Paul of Acts.

Whatever the source, it seems Paul's travels were clearly not carefully planned.

The Paul of the epistles makes and breaks promises, he changes his mind, he stays longer, and he cuts his visits short. He even loses his co-travelers, because he changes his mind and forgets where he sent them.

What is clear, from both Acts and from Paul's own writings, is that in the early years of his missionary work Paul always traveled with Barnabas.

Whether or not it was the case in those earliest days, or if it was a pattern that developed later, Paul had many disciples who worked with him and traveled with him. We know them by the names of Titus, Timothy, Silvanus, Sosthenes, Phoebe, Junia, Apollos, Priscia, and Aquila.

Often, he would send one or a few of them ahead to whatever city, for Paul traveled exclusively to Roman cities, he was going next, with a letter introducing Paul and his mission. These disciples would spend their time, awaiting Paul's arrival, getting to know the local Christians who could be expected to give Paul and his companions somewhere to stay, and finding Paul work in one of the city's workshops.

These were not quite factories, but rather small places of production where raw materials or partially finished products were worked by several skilled artisans into a final product. Many workshops worked on commissions, so there would be a mix of people coming through, from slaves to wealthy customers.

When Paul finally arrived, this meant that he had somewhere to go, and some way to support himself, while preaching in the evenings, and even in the days to his coworkers and the customers visiting the workshop.

After having planted a small cell of a Christian community in a city, Paul often moved on, and kept in touch with his new church through letters, delivered by one of his trusted disciples.

The oldest such letter that still exists is the First Epistle to the Thessalonians, which Paul wrote less than a year after establishing the community there. The traditional view of three apostolic tours would place this visit during Paul's second journey.

According to Acts 17, Paul converted many Gentiles in Thessaloniki, including some very prominent Greek women, but his preaching at the synagogue left him very unpopular with the Jews. The angry Jewish mob forced Paul to flee for his life. His failure to convert the Jews of Thessaloniki becomes evident as we read Paul's letter. He greets the Thessalonians as former idol worshipers, which identifies them as a group consisting entirely of Gentiles.

We also learn from Acts that by the time that this journey to Thessaloniki was undertaken, Paul and Barnabas had gone their separate ways. It started with an argument, before Paul left Antioch. The pair had previously taken Mark the Evangelist, the cousin of Barnabas, with them on their travels, but Mark had left them on the road to go back to Jerusalem. Paul did not want to travel with Mark again, but Barnabas would not travel without him.

Paul is often known as the Apostle to the Gentiles. Although he did proselytize among the Jews, he seems to have seen it as his particular calling to spread the word of God among the nations, so as to fulfill the ancient Jewish apocalyptic prophecy that in the end days, all the nations would seek God through Israel.

Perhaps this was because the Gentiles were more predisposed to accepting Paul's Gospel. The Jews were guarded against those foreign idolaters whom Paul was so willing to include, and were expecting a Messiah who would literally become their king and lead the tribes of Israel to glory. Paul's message of salvation after death was much closer to the popular Pagan mystery cults of the day. In the Acts of the Apostles, we see Paul several times washing his hands off the fate of the Jews, and turning to the less hostile Gentiles.

Paul's Controversies

While Paul was busy spreading the Gospel among the Gentiles of the eastern Mediterranean, a debate was growing in Jerusalem.

It was fourteen years after Paul's experience on the road to Damascus, approximately in the year 49 or 50 AD, that he returned to Jerusalem to speak to the original Apostles. Paul tells us, in Galatians 2, that he went with Barnabas, whom he had not yet split from, and his disciple Titus.

In Jerusalem they met with Peter, James, and John and presented to them the Gospel they had been spreading among the Gentiles during their travels. The three approved, and it was agreed that Paul and Barnabas would continue to act specifically as disciples to the Gentiles.

It was these Gentiles that were the cause of so much controversy and debate in Jerusalem, and in Christian communities around the Mediterranean, at the time.

While Gentiles had originally been allowed to enter into the Christian community without a full conversion to Judaism, that is to say: without going through circumcision, and without following the strict Mosaic laws of purity, there were an increasing number of Jewish Christians who were discontented by this arrangement. Acts 15 tells us that the visit of Paul and Barnabas in Jerusalem around 49-50 AD was in fact as official ambassadors to speak on behalf of the Gentiles on a council to decide, once and for all, the early church's official stance on circumcision and the law of Moses.

Paul and Barnabas won the argument and the result, we learn, was that a letter was sent out to the Christian communities instructing them about the decision: "It is the decision of the Holy Spirit and of us not to place on you any burden beyond these necessities, namely, to abstain from meat sacrificed to idols, from blood, from meats of strangled animals, and from unlawful marriage. If you keep free of these, you will be doing what is right." (Acts 15:28-29)

Whether there was in fact a Council of Jerusalem has long been debated by historians. One important argument against such a council comes from the writings of Paul himself. When Paul wrote to the Galatians about that apparently fateful visit to Jerusalem, he did not mention participating in any such important debate. Instead, he tells us that he was approved to preach to the Gentiles. The next event that Paul tells us of is his conflict with Peter in Antioch, on another topic of Mosaic law. Why would Paul leave out such crucially important details, when he clearly did not mind telling the Galatians that he had been in conflict with the Twelve?

Regardless of the historicity of the Council of Jerusalem, these passages bring to our attention that there was a very real conflict going on, splitting the Christian community in two.

Not long after Paul had returned to Antioch, the Apostle Peter came to visit. When he arrived, Peter dined often with the Gentiles during their communal meals. After some time, however, they were joined by some

Jewish Christians sent to Antioch by James. Suddenly, Peter would no longer dine with the Gentiles and there were many others who saw his change and followed suit. Although it is not explicitly stated, the problem was most likely that the Gentile diet was not kosher and the Jews who dined with them were thus breaking Mosaic Law, but there might have been further underlying issues concerning circumcision and Jewish Law.

Regardless of their reasons, Paul was outraged by their actions. It was Paul's opinion that through the coming of Christ the righteous were righteous through their faith in Christ rather than through their maintaining of the ancient Jewish laws. When Isaiah prophesied that all peoples would seek God through Israel, Paul felt, it meant that they would come to God as Gentiles, not as Israelites.

This attempt to force Gentiles to act like Jews went against the prophecy, and Paul's perception of the message of Christ. Furthermore, changing sides out of fear of losing one's more orthodox supporters, Paul felt, was pure hypocrisy. He called Peter out publicly, but in the end it was Peter and James' fraction who won the argument and as a result the group of Jewish Christians favoring Gentile circumcision and adoption of Mosaic Laws grew significantly in Antioch. Even Paul's long term friend and companion, Barnabas, took the side of Peter and James, which may have facilitated their split very soon thereafter.

Unfortunately, it was not merely in Jerusalem and in Antioch that the fractions were felt and Paul was met by early Christian controversy. It also occurred in the communities that he had established abroad, especially in his absence.

One such controversy is on display in 1 Corinthians, the letter that Paul wrote to his church in Corinth in response to a letter he had received from them. In this epistle we see Paul appealing to his community to be one in Christ, for they had split into fractions. Some said to follow Paul, others to follow his co-missionary Apollos, others still followed Peter.

The rift was probably largely caused by the stream of missionaries traveling through Corinth. They were Jewish Christians, who preached, according to Paul, another Jesus and "a different Gospel," and they proclaimed that Paul was a false Apostle, sent by Satan, proclaiming a weak Jesus. Given the increase in followers of Peter it is possible that some of them belonged to the fraction wanting all Gentiles to follow Mosaic Law, but they could also have belonged to other fractions. They were very influential, and their hold over the congregation in Corinth did not end with a single letter from Paul. His first letter was not well-received, nor his second, third or fourth.

When Paul then finally arrived in Corinth to address the matter in person, he walked right into a confrontation. At full assembly, a powerful local believer condemned Paul with devastating force, publicly humiliating him. Paul fled humiliated, and from a safe distance he fired off an angry letter, known as the "letter of tears," which he sent Titus to deliver. This fifth letter, the fourth that is partially preserved in the Bible, can be found in 2 Corinthians 10-13. The result of Paul's "letter of tears" was that Titus was eventually welcomed back into Corinth, and the person who had publicly attacked Paul was rebuked. But, the warlike nature of Paul's words forever hurt the relationship between Paul and the congregation.

Not long after his "letter of tears," Paul found himself in prison. He had been preaching the Gospel in Ephesus when he had some trouble with a competing Christian fraction and ended up imprisoned. He alludes to this in Philippians 1.

Imprisonment in the Roman Empire was rarely a final punishment, and there were no real public prisons, but rather it was an incarceration awaiting a trial, usually within a military buildings or a large household. While under lock and guard, Paul was allowed visitors, even to baptize them, financial assistance, and to send letters. One letter to the Philippians thanked them for sending money, probably as a bribe to keep up Paul's many privileges.

According to the late 2nd century Saint Paul and the Baptized Lion, Paul was not merely imprisoned in Ephesus, but sentenced to death by fighting wild animals in the arena. Paul only escaped with the help of a friendly lion, whom Paul had previously baptized.

When Paul was released from his imprisonment in Ephesus, Paul immediately wrote a letter to Corinth to express his happiness over their reconciliation and to promise them a visit. He finally arrived in circa 57 AD, a man in his early to mid-50s, approximately five years after his first visit. He had regained some of his former respect, and could enjoy a level of authority within the community.

It was not an extended visit and he soon bid them farewell again. When he left, he took with him several sealed bags of coins. This was the Gentiles' collection as a gift to the poor of Jerusalem, honoring a promise Paul had made to Peter, John and James on the day that they approved his mission to the Gentiles. It may also have contained their collection in order to offer sacrifice at the Temple. It was also common practice for the Jewish diaspora to make such collections for temple sacrifices in their absence. It was not only the Jews who acted in this way, many Pagan diaspora communities in the Roman empire are known to have sent money back to the temple of their hometown's god.

Paul's Final Years

Paul sailed to Jerusalem with the money, probably from Cenchreae where he had been staying with Phoebe, a convert who ran a church from her house there. Phoebe, on the other hand set off to Rome as Paul's delegation to the Christians there, with a letter of introduction introducing Paul and his gospel. This letter is preserved as Paul's Epistle to the Romans, in which Paul promised to visit the Roman Christians on his way to Spain, where he hoped to found new Christian communities.

According to the writer of Acts, Paul had received warning through the Holy Spirit that things would not go well for him in Jerusalem. In Acts 20, Paul tells the Ephesians: "But now, compelled by the Spirit, I am going to Jerusalem. What will happen to me there I do not know, except that in one city after another the Holy Spirit has been warning me that imprisonment and hardships await me. Yet I consider life of no importance to me, if only I may finish my course and the ministry that I received from the Lord Jesus, to bear witness to the gospel of God's grace."

In Acts 21, he was warned by the Holy Spirit, through the people of Tyre, as well as by a prophet in Caesarea, and when he arrived in Jerusalem he was warned by James and urged to purify himself so that no one could accuse him of being an unlawful Jew. Many Bible scholars see this as part of the Acts author's attempt to liken Paul's story to the Passion of Christ. In his own writings, as we have just seen, Paul seems oblivious to the danger that awaits in Jerusalem, and even makes plans for trips to follow.

The main source for information about what happened next is Acts 21-28, although historians doubt the historicity of the events described. According to acts, some Jews from the provinces of Minor Asia stirred up a mob and seized Paul inside the Temple, accusing him of having brought Gentiles into the sacred Court of Israel, where only Hebrews were allowed. Although the author of Acts makes it clear that this was a false accusation based on a simple misunderstanding, some scholars believe that the allegations were in fact true.

The allegations against Paul are so inconvenient for his supporters, they mean to say, that they can hardly have been made up simply for the sake of making Paul into a martyr. And, if it was true that the allegations were made, they also feel that it was plausible that they were correct. They argue that when Paul originally delivered his Gospel to Peter, James, and John, he did so in the presence of an uncircumcised Greek Christian. These same historians feel that Paul most likely planned to do the same thing in the Temple, a very provocative move in favor of his inclusive understanding of the Gospel.

While the Jews at the Temple tried to kill Paul, word reached the local Roman cohort commander that all of Jerusalem was in a riot, so he immediately charged upon the mob with several soldiers. Paul was arrested. After being questioned by the commander, Paul was allowed to address the Jews in Hebrew, and although they listened they still wished him dead.

The commander ordered that Paul be interrogated under the lash to determine why it was the Jews wanted him dead. When they had bound Paul, stretched for the whip, Paul remarked to the centurion on duty that it would probably not be lawful for them to whip a Roman citizen like himself. This sudden claim of Roman citizenship, at just the right moment, and the subsequent unquestioning trust of Paul by all Romans, has lead many scholars to question this part of the story.

At the moment of his arrest, Paul had told the commander "I am a Jew, of Tarsus in Cilicia, a citizen of no mean city." If his historically very unlikely Roman citizenship were more than a literary device, why would he not have included his Roman citizenship in his presentation of himself?

Next, Paul was allowed to address the Sanhedrin, the Jewish court at Jerusalem. His speech caused such an uproar that several men created a plot to kill Paul. The Roman commander in charge then sent Paul to Caesarea, where the governor held him prisoner for two more years until a new governor was appointed.

The new governor wished to ingratiate himself with the Jews, so he ordered that Paul be sent back to Jerusalem to stand trial before the Jews, but as a Roman citizen, and unwilling to go back to a certain stoning, Paul demanded to be allowed to plead his case before the Emperor in Rome. Before setting off, however, he was allowed to plea his case before King Herod Agrippa II, the Roman client king of Galilee.

Traveling to Rome was a slow affair even by sea, as seafarers in Antiquity preferred to sail close to the shore rather than go out too far across the open water. It was also a dangerous affair, and before they could arrive in Rome the ship that was taking Paul across shipwrecked on Malta, where the islanders were very kind to him. He finally reached Rome, circa 60 AD, about 55 years old.

His imprisonment in Rome was probably not terribly difficult for him. Paul was allowed to live on his own in a sort of house arrest, with a soldier present to ensure that he did not try to leave the city. And as Acts 28 tells us: "He remained for two full years in his lodgings. He received all who came to him, and with complete assurance and without hindrance he proclaimed the kingdom of God and taught about the Lord Jesus Christ."

What happened next is the matter of some debate. The now traditional view, which exists in several versions, is that Paul stood trial before Emperor Nero, was found guilty, and finally beheaded. Those familiar with the martyrdom of Saint Peter may wonder why Paul was not crucified, like his fellow Apostle, and the reason for this was that Paul was supposedly a Roman citizen. Crucifixion was a slow and painful death, reserved for foreigners.

According to The Martyrdom of Saint Paul, this trial came about because Paul bought a barn outside of Rome in order to preach to the people. A great many people came to see him, and among them were

Nero's favorite cup bearer, Patroclus.

The boy, alas, sat on a high window to better hear Paul and fell to his death purely by accident. When Paul raised the boy from death, he was overjoyed and ran back to his master, proclaiming that he had enlisted as a "soldier" in the coming "Kingdom."

A coming kingdom with soldiers frightened Nero, who arrested and executed all Christians he could find. Paul was the first to die, but when he was beheaded it was milk, rather than blood, that gushed out of Paul's neck. Resurrected, Paul later returned to rebuke Nero for breaking both divine and Roman law, and so Nero released all of the Christians.

The fourth century Passion of Saint Paul tells us that before his beheading, Paul borrowed the veil of a woman called Plautilla as a blindfold. He returned it to her after his resurrection.

Some sources claim that Paul never died in Rome at all. The Acts of Peter and the Acts of Xanthippe and Polyxena maintain that after his imprisonment in Rome, Paul went on to proselytize in the west, like he planned to in his letter to the Romans. Other sources claim that he returned eastwards, for yet an apostolic tour.

From Greek Apostle to Roman Saint

Although Paul was clearly an important figure in the early Christian community during his lifetime, it was in the centuries following his death that his role in the church, especially in the Roman Catholic Church, was solidified.

If Saint Paul died in Rome, it can be assumed that he was also buried there. Yet, the earliest written source for Paul's burial place was written 160 years after his death. The source is Eusebius of Caesarea's Ecclesiastical History, which states that the body of Paul was interred just outside of Rome. The lateness of this source does not mean, of course, that there was no truth to it. The fact that no one had written about it earlier may simply speak of an increased interest in Paul's burial place in the third century.

The sixth century Passion of the Holy Apostles Peter and Paul claims that Paul's and Peter's burials in Rome were no easy affairs. Christians from the eastern Roman Empire, that is to say the Greek speaking Christians whom Paul had once proselytized amongst, tried to steal the bodies of the martyred saints.

The plot was discovered, however, and the Christians at Rome buried the two saints temporarily in the Catacombs on the Appian Way. When the danger of ambush was over, they moved the bodies to their permanent location. For Saint Peter, this of course meant the Vatican, but for Paul that meant his shrine, and later Basilica, on the Ostian Way just outside of Rome.

Some time in between the writings of Eusebius and the sixth century Latin passion story, Christianity had been adopted by the Roman emperors and received official status as a fundamentally Roman religion. It followed that the veneration of Saint Paul, a church father who after all was said to be Roman and was thought to be buried in Rome, received imperial sponsorship.

In a sense, Paul and Peter came to replace the Pagan divine fathers of the city, Romulus and Remus. Prudentius, the great 4th century Roman Christian poet, envisioned Paul more like an Aenaeas, the Trojan hero who fled the burning city of Troy and founded the city of Rome – he came from Asia Minor to Rome to found a better Christendom.

Even Paul's early veneration followed the Roman pagan customs, of celebrating the grateful dead with a physical feast at their tombs. The grateful dead were expected to participate in this feast, and archeology shows us that Paul's marble sarcophagus made for Paul in the 4th century had a hole for a feeding tube, so that his remains could be fed.

In the place on the Ostian Way where Paul was venerated, Emperor Theodosius founded in the 4th century a great Basilica, containing several relics of Paul: a bloodstained shroud, his ashes and his bones, as well as a shrine with adapted Roman military laurels and athletic trophies. People traveled from far and wide to see Paul's relics, and to receive miraculous healings from them. The Basilica stood largely intact until 1823, when it was taken down in a fire. The Church of Saint Paul Outside-the-Walls replaced it in 1854.

In 2006, Paul's marble sarcophagus was rediscovered by archaeologists underneath the main altar, beneath a slab with the inscription "Paulo apostolo mart," Latin for "Paul the Apostle, Martyr." The bone fragments inside were carbon dated and found to derive from the 1st or 2nd century, which Pope Benedict XVI has taken to mean that they are in fact the mortal remains of Saint Paul.

But Paul was never a purely Roman Saint. As early as in the 180s, one hundred years before any mention of his burial in Rome, the <u>Acts of the Scillitan Martyrs</u> makes mention of the North African Christians having access to "books and letters of a just man named Paul."

Still today Paul is revered in all Christian denominations, both eastern and western. In the Roman Catholic Church, his conversion is celebrated on January 25 and his martyrdom with Saint Peter is honored on June 29.

Prayers to Saint Paul

Prayer for Priests

Great convert and Apostle of the Gentiles,

you became Christlike
and knew only Christ Crucified.
Though extremely learned,
you relied completely on the Wisdom received
from the Spirit
and taught from the abundance of your heart.
Instruct modern [priests and] evangelists
those who preach Christ to others.
Let them realize that their actions
speak louder than any words they may use.
Teach them to use their talents
in conveying their God, given message
but to rely above all on the promptings of the Spirit.

Amen.

Prayer for Priests II

St. Paul, great Apostle of the Gentiles,

intercede for us to God
[in favor of our priests].
You are God's special vessel of election.
Through your intercession
we hope to receive from Him this special grace:
(here make your request)
[mentioning the name of the priest you pray for,
his ministry,
his spiritual life,
and his intentions].

God, you have instructed many nations
through the preaching of the Apostle Paul.
Let the power of his intercession with You help us
[and our priest]
who venerate his memory this day.

Amen.

Prayer for Priests III

O Glorious Saint Paul,

after persecuting the Church
you became by God's grace its most zealous Apostle.
To carry the knowledge of Jesus,
our Divine Savior,
to the uttermost parts of the earth
you joyfully endured prison,
scourgings, stonings, and shipwreck,
as well as all manner of persecutions
culminating in the shedding of the last drop of your blood
for our Lord Jesus Christ.

[May your example inspire priests today
to be zealous in their service to God's people.]

Obtain for our priests
the grace to labor strenuously
to bring the faith to others
and to accept any trials and tribulations
that may come their way.
Help them to be inspired by your Epistles
and to partake of your indomitable love for Jesus,
so that after they have finished their course
they may join you in praising him in heaven for all eternity.

Amen.

Prayer for Patience

O glorious St. Paul,

who from a persecutor of Christianity,
did become a most ardent apostle of zeal;
and who to make known the Saviour Jesus Christ
to the ends of the world did suffer with joy imprisonment,
scourging, stonings, shipwrecks
and persecutions of every kind,
and in the end did shed your blood to the last drop,
obtain for us the grace to receive,
as favours of the Divine Mercy,
infirmities, tribulations,
and mistfortunes of the present life,
so that the vicissitudes of this our exile
will not render us cold in the service of God,
but will render us always more faithful and fervent.

Amen.

Prayer for Inspiration

OGlorious Saint Paul, after persecuting the Church you became by God's grace its most zealous Apostle. To carry the knowledge of Jesus, our divine Savior, to the uttermost parts of the earth you joyfully endured prison, scourgings, stonings, and shipwreck, as well as all manner of persecutions culminating in the shedding of the last drop of your blood for our Lord Jesus Christ.

Obtain for us the grace to labor strenuously to being the faith to others and to accept any trials and tribulations that may come our way. Help us to be inspired by your Epistles and to partake of your indomitable love for Jesus, so that after we have finished our course we may join you in praising him in heaven for all eternity. Amen.

Prayer for Action

Great convert and Apostle of the Gentiles, you became Christlike and knew only Christ Crucified. Though extremely learned, you relied completely on the Wisdom received from the Spirit and taught from the abundance of your heart. Instruct modern evangelists - those who preach Christ to others. Let them realize that their actions speak louder than any words they may use. Teach them to use their talents in conveying their God-given message but to rely above all on the promptings of the Spirit. Amen.

Made in the USA
Las Vegas, NV
25 October 2024

10343531R00039